W9-BUY-023

World Heritage in
CAPPADOCIA

Murat Ertuğrul GÜLYAZ
Archaeologist

7. EDITION 2013 - Istanbul

CONTENTS

Text   : Murat E. GÜLYAZ (mgulyaz@hotmail.com)
Photos   : Murat E. GÜLYAZ
Translation   : Sevim KARABIYIK-Gerald BODEY
Illustrations   : Çağdaş ŞAHİN, Efkan BEYAZ
Cover Desing   : Ahmet ÖZYURT
Publisher   : Ünal İKİZOĞLU (0 532 684 39 88)
Printing   : Seçil Ofset /İstanbul
Distribitors   : Digital Dünyası
                  (unalikizoglu@gmail.com)
                Tel   : 0 384 214 37 77-
                Fax   : 0 384 214 37 76

ISBN   : 978-605-61561-4-4

© *All rights are the property of the author. Not to be copied or repro-
duced without permission.*

3

Erciyes

THE LOCATION OF CAPPADOCIA

In his 17 volume book "Geographika" written during the reign of Roman Emperor Augustus, Strabon, a writer of antiquity, describes the borders of the Cappadocian Region as a very large area surrounded by the Taurus Mountains in the south, by Aksaray in the west, Malatya in the east and all the way up to the Black Sea coast in the north. However, present day Cappadocia is the area covered by the city provinces of Nevşehir, Aksaray, Niğde, Kayseri and Kırşehir. The smaller rocky region of Cappadocia is the area around Uçhisar, Göreme, Avanos, Ürgüp, Derinkuyu, Kaymaklı and Ihlara.

VOLCANIC ERUPTIONS AND GEOLOGICAL FORMATIONS
Rock Structures

Mount Erciyes, Hasandağ and Göllüdağ were active volcanoes in early geological periods. Alongside many other volcanoes, eruptions of these volcanoes started in the Early Miocene Era (10 million years ago) and have continued until the present day.

The lava produced by these volcanoes, under the Neogen lakes, formed a layer of tufa on the area's plateaus, which varied in hardness and in thickness from 100 to 150m. The substances in the layers include ignimbrite, soft tufa, tufa, lahar, ash, clay, sandstone, marn, basalt and other agglomerates.

Plateaus, mostly shaped by the lava of the bigger volcanoes, were continuously altered by the eruptions of smaller volcanoes. Starting in the Early Pliocene Period, the rivers in the area, especially the Kızılırmak (Red River) and local lakes, contributed to the erosion of this layer of tufa stone, eventually giving the area its present day shape.

Kızılçukur Valley

Formation of Fairy Chimneys

The interesting rock formations known as "fairy chimneys," were formed as the result of the erosion of the tufa layer, sculpted by wind and floodwater running down the slopes of the valleys. Water found its way through the valleys, creating cracks and ruptures in the hard rock. The softer, easily erodible material underneath was gradually swept away. The slopes then receded, and in this way, conical formations protected with basalt caps were created. The fairy chimneys with caps, mainly found in the vicinity of Ürgüp, have a conical shaped body with a boulder on top of it. The cone is constructed of tufa and volcanic ash, while the cap is made up of hard, more resistant rock such as lahar or ignimbrite. Various types of fairy chimneys are found in Cappadocia. Among these are those with caps, cones, mushroom-like formations, columns, and pointed rocks.

Fairy chimneys are generally found in the valleys of the Uçhisar- Ürgüp- Avanos triangle. Some are located between Ürgüp and Sahinefendi, and around the town of Çat in Nevşehir.

Others can be found in the Soğanlı valley in Kayseri, and in the village of Selime in Aksaray. Another characteristic feature of the area is the sweeping curves and patterns on the sides of the valleys, formed by rainwater. The layers of sedimentation exposed by erosion, display a range of hues.

The array of colors seen in some of the valleys is due to the difference in the heat of the lava layers as they formed. Such patterns can be seen in Uçhisar, Çavuşin/Güllüdere, Göreme/Meskendir, Ortahisar/Kızılçukur and Pancarlık valleys.

Paşabağları/Avanos

Kılıçlar Valley/Göreme

CAPPADOCIA IN THE PREHISTORIC PERIODS

Prehistoric Period

Evidence of Prehistoric cultures in Cappadocia can most easily be found around Köşkhöyük/Niğde, Aşıklıhöyük/Aksaray, and in the Civelek cave near Nevşehir. Excavations in these three areas are still taking place.

Civelek Cave

Civelek cave is in the vicinity of Civelek village, situated 4km west of Gülşehir, in the province of Nevşehir. The cave is found in the hill known as Gurlek Hill. Access to the cave can be gained by means of a gallery, which extends downwards for 14m into the limestone cave. There are many calcite crystal stalactites between 5 and 15cm in length, hanging from the sections of the cave ceiling. The main part of this ceiling is 22 by 11m.

During excavations carried out by Nevşehir Museum and cave experts from Italy, hand made cups, cooking pots of various sizes, spindles, and tools made from stone and bone dating from the Chalcolithic Period (5500- 3000 BC) were unearthed from the floor of the cave, and especially among the collapsed rocks. In addition to this excavation, surface excavations in the surrounding caves unearthed tools made from obsidian and flint. In an attempt at preservation, Civelek cave is closed to visitors.

Aşıklı Höyük (mound)

Archaeological excavations discovered the first brick living quarters in Cappadocia in Aşıklı Höyük (mound), an extension of Aksaray's Ihlara Valley settlements.

Yellow and pink clay plaster was used to make the walls and floors of the houses.

Finds from Civelek Cave/Chalcolithic Period

Aşıklı Höyük/Selime (Mihriban Özbaşaran)

These are some of the most beautiful and complicated architectural examples of the first towns.

The dead of this area were buried in the hocker (like a fetus) position, like a fetus in the womb, on the floor of their houses. According to Prof. U. Esin, who re-searched at Aşıklı Höyük, a population greater than had been previously theorized is revealed by the abun-dance and density of the settlements in the areas in the Aceramic Neolithic Period. Nowhere else in Anatolia can the unique obsidian tools be found, like those from this Cappadocian mound.

Figurines made from lightly baked clay were un-earthed together with flat stone axes wrought in many fine shapes. Chisels and coulters made from bones, and ornaments made from copper, agate and other differ-ent kinds of stones were also found. Evidence provid-ed by a skeleton found here indicates that the earliest brain surgery (trepanation) known in the world was performed on a woman 20-25 years of age at Aşıklı Höyük.

General view of Kültepe Kanesh Karum

CAPPADOCIA IN THE HISTORIC PERIODS
Pro-Hittite and Assyrian Trade Colonies (3000BC - 1750BC)

Mining reached its peak of development in Anatolia during the Early Bronze Age. Major developments were observed in Northern Anatolia towards the end of this period. Between 2000BC and 1750BC, Assyrian merchants from northern Mesopotamia formed the first commercial organizations by establishing trade colonies in Anatolia. The center of these colonies was at Kanesh Kharum near Kültepe in Kayseri province. Another important commercial market place, which was referred to in documents, is the Kharum Hattush at Boğazköy.

Anatolia was rich in gold, silver, and copper, but lacked tin, which was essential for the manufacturing of bronze as an alloy. For this reason, tin was one of the major trading materials, as well as textile goods and perfumes.

The merchants had no political dominance, but were protected by the regional rulers. Thanks to the Assyrian merchants, writing was also seen for the first time in Anatolian in this period.

From the "Cappadocia tablets", cuneiform clay tablets on which ancient Assyrian was written, it was learned that merchants paid a 10% road tax to the ruler, received a 30% interest from their debtors, and paid a 5% tax to the Anatolian kings for goods they sold.

The same tablets tell us that they sometimes married Anatolian women, and the marriage agreements contained clauses to protect the women's rights against their husbands.

Assyrian merchants also introduced cylinder seals, metallurgy, their religious beliefs, gods, and temples to Anatolia. Native Anatolian art flourished under the influence of Assyrian Mesopotamian art, eventually developing an identity of its own. During the following ages this developed into the fundamentals of Hittite art.

Cuneiform clay tablet/Kültepe Kanesh Kharum

Rituel vessel from Kültepe Kanesh Kharum
Kayseri Museum

The golden diadem and the eye annd mouth plates left in
Kanesh Kharum's grave as the gifts to dead./
Kayseri Museum

Idol/Kültepe Kanesh Kharum

11

Hittite Period (1750-1200 BC)

The Hittites, coming from Europe via the Causcasus, and settling in Cappadocia around 2000BC, formed an empire in the region merging with the native people of the area. Their language was of Indo-European origin.

The capital of the Hittite kingdom was at Hattushash (Bogazkoy), and the other important cities were Alacahöyük and Alisar. In the Cappadocia region, engraved stone monuments dating back from the Imperial Period can be found near water sources and strategic routes.

By means of these rock monuments, the routes used by the Hittite kings to reach the southern countries can be determined. Within the borders of Kayseri, located to the south of Mount Erciyes, are the rock monuments of Fraktin, Taşçı and İmamkulu. They served several purposes; they were intended to venerate the gods, to show the gratitude of the great King (Hattusili III) and Queen (Puduhepa) to the gods; as well as to show the extent of the Empire's power.

A golden plate with a Hittite God relief/ Kültepe Kanesh Kharum-Kayseri Museum

Late Hittite Settlement in Göllüdağ

12

Late Hittite rock monument from Sivasa/Gülşehir

Late Hittite Kingdom (1200-700 BC)

After the Phrygians destroyed all the important towns in Central Anatolia eliminating the Hittite Empire, fragments of the Late Hittite Kingdoms sprang up around central and Southeast Anatolia. The Late Hittite Kingdom in Cappadocia was the Tabal kingdom, which extended over Kayseri, Nevşehir and Niğde.

Rock monuments from this age, with Hittite hieroglyphics can be found at Gülşehir-Sivasa (Gökçetoprak), Acıgöl-Topada, and Hacıbektaş-Karaburna.

Fraktin Kaya Anıtı/Kayseri

13

Persian Period and The Kingdom of Cappadocia (585BC-332BC)

The Cimmerians ended the Phrygian reign in Anatolia, and were then followed by the Medes (585BC) and the Persians (525BC). The Persians divided the empire into semi-autonomous provinces and ruled the area, using governors who were known as "Satraps".

In the ancient Persian language, Katpatuka, the word for Cappadocia, meant "Land of the well bred horses". Since the religion they were devoted to was the Zoroastrian religion and fire was considered to be divine, the volcanoes in the area, Erciyes and Hasandağ were sacred for them.

The Persians constructed a "Royal Road" connecting their capital city to the Aegean region passing through Cappadocia. The Macedonian King Alexander defeated Persian armies twice, in 334 and 332 B.C., and conquered this great Empire.

After bringing the Persian Empire to an end, King Alexander met with great resistance in Cappadocia. When Alexander tried to rule the region through one of his commanders named Sabictus, the people resisted and declared Ariarthes, a Persian aristocrat, king. As an industrious ruler, Ariarthes I (332 - 322 B.C.) extended the borders of the Cappadocian kingdom. The kingdom of Cappadocia lived in peace until the death of Alexander.

From then until 17AD, when it became a Roman province, it fought wars with the Macedonians, the Galatians, the Pontus nation and the Romans.

Herakles Sargophagus/Kayseri Museum

14

Roman Period (17AD - 395AD)

The wars came to an end in 17AD when Tiberius conquered Cappadocia and placed it under Roman rule. After the conquest, the Romans reconstructed the road to the west, which was of both commercial and military significance.

During the Roman Period, in the area many migrations occurred, as well as attacks from the east. Roman military units known as "Legions" defended the area. During the reign of Emperor Septimus Severus Cappadocia's economy flourished, but later the capital, Kayseri (Caesera) was attacked by Sassanid armies from Iran. Emperor Gordianus III ordered the construction of defensive city walls.

During this time some of the first Christians were moving from the big cities to villages. In the 4th century, when Kayseri was a flourishing religious centre, the rocky surroundings of Göreme were discovered. The Christians adopted the teachings of St. Basil, Bishop of Caesarea (Kayseri), and began to lead a monastic life in the carved out cliffs and fairy chimneys of Cappadocia.

Tyana/Niğde

15

Byzantine Period (397AD - 1071AD)

When the Roman Empire divided into west and east, Cappadocia fell under the Eastern Roman Empire. In the early 7th century there were severe wars between the Sassanid and Byzantine armies, and for 6 or 7 years the Sassanids held the area. In 651 Caliph Omer ended the domination of the Sassanids, and the Arab Ommiades began to attack.

Long lasting religious debates among Christian sects reached a peak with the adoption of the Iconoclastic position by Leon III, who was influenced by Islamic traditions. Christian priests and monks who were in favour of icons began to take refuge in Cappadocia.

The Iconoclastic period lasted over a century (726-843). During this time although several Cappadocian churches were under the influence of iconoclasm, the people who were in favor of icons were able to continue to worship comfortably.

Gümüşler Monastery/Niğde

A female mummy from the Early Christian Period/Niğde Museum

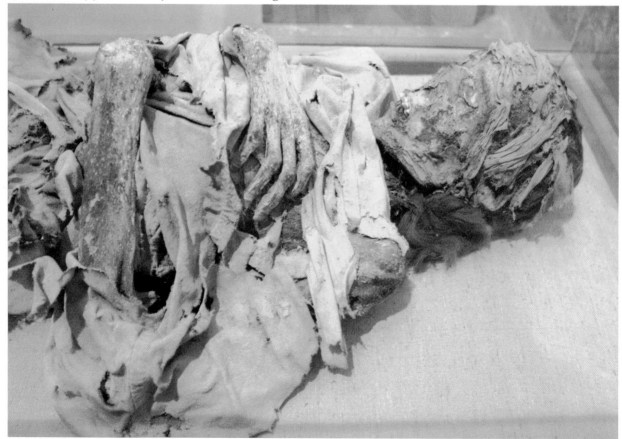

Seljuk Period (1071-1299)

The native land of the Seljuks, established by Seljuk Bey from Oğuz Turks, was central Asia. The Seljuks, who converted to Islam spreading towards north in the 10th century, tried to extend their power fighting against the tribes, which had not been converted.

The defeat and the capture of the Byzantine Emperor Romanos Diogenes in 1071 by Alparslan, the great grandson of Seljuk Bey, resulted in the decline of the Byzantine Empire and the beginning of a new era in the history of Anatolia. In 1075 the Anatolian Seljuk State was founded. In 1082 Kayseri was conquered by Turks and Cappadocia came under Seljuk rule.

Anatolia, which was an important region where Christianity had spread, became part of Islamic world, which covered a large area; from North Africa, to Middle Asia and to the Near East. The conquest of Anatolia by Seljuk Turks did not influence the administrative authority of the Christian patriarchy.

We know this because in inscriptions from the 13th century found in the church of St George in the Ihlara region, names of the Seljuk Sultan Mesud II and the Byzantine Emperor Andronicus are treated with admiration.

As a result of the decline of the Anatolian Seljuk State at the end of the 13th century, small beyliks (domains of minor rulers) came into being in different parts of Anatolia. In 1308, the Ilkhanids, of Mongolian origin, invaded Anatolia and destroyed Kayseri, one of the important cities in the Cappadocia Region. Seljuk Sultans were controlled by the Mongolians and could not act independently. From then on, Anatolia was administered by the beyliks founded by different Turkish tribes.

Alaaddin Mosque-Niğde

Ottoman Period

The Region of Cappadocia was very peaceful also during the Ottoman Period. Nevşehir was a small village in the province of Niğde until the time of Damat İbrahim Pasha. At the beginning of the 18th century, especially during the time of Damat İbrahim Pasha, places like Nevşehir, Gülşehir, Özkonak, Avanos and Ürgüp prospered and mosques, külliyes (a collection of buildings of an institution, usually composed of schools, a mosque, mental institutions, hospital, kitchen, etc.) and fountains were built.

The bridge in the centre of the town of Özkonak, which was built during Yavuz Sultan Selim's campaign to the east (1514), is an important example of an early Ottoman Period building in the province of Nevşehir. The Christian people living in the area were treated with tolerance in the Ottoman Period as they had been in the Seljuk Period.

The 18th century church of Constantine-Helena in Sinasos-Ürgüp, the 19th century church built in honor of Dimitrius in Gülşehir and the Orthodox Church in Derinkuyu are some of the best examples of this tolerance.

Kurşunlu Mosque/Nevşehir

NATURAL, HISTORICAL AND RELIGIOUS CENTRES OF CAPPADOCIA

Uçhisar

Uçhisar is situated at the highest point in the region, on the Nevşehir-Göreme road, just 7km from Nevşehir. It is not known when Uçhisar was first inhabited, however, in style, it resembles Ortahisar and the Selime Kalesi (castle) in the Ihlara Region.

The top of the citadel provides a magnificent panorama of the surrounding area. Many rooms hollowed out into the rock are connected to each other with stairs, tunnels and passages. At the entrances of the rooms, there are millstone doors, just like the ones in the underground settlements, used to control access to these places. Due to the erosion in places of this multi-leveled castle, it is unfortunately not possible to reach all of the rooms.

The fairy chimneys to the west, east and north of Uçhisar were hollowed out and used as graves during the Roman period. Inside these rock-cut tombs, the entrances of which generally face west, are klines or stone slabs on which the bodies were laid.

Many rock cut churches have been discovered not only on the skirts of the castle but also inside it. The reason for this may be the fact that Göreme, having numerous churches and monasteries, is very close to Uçhisar.

The simple Byzantine graves on top of the castle are not very interesting due to the fact that they have been eroded and ransacked. It is said that in towns with citadels, such as Uçhisar, Ortahisar and Ürgüp (Başhisar), long defence tunnels reached far into the surrounding areas. However, since the tunnels have collapsed in places, this theory cannot be confirmed, but is a popular myth due to the great distances they cover.

In addition to the tombs, many dove-cotes were hollowed out into the castle, in fairy chimneys around it and on the cliff faces. The local farmers, although they did not have much land, were in need of good crops. Knowing that dove excrement could help them with this problem and increase the amount of crops they would harvest, farmers hollowed out dove-cotes into the sides of fairy chimneys and on the cliff faces. Later the fertilizer was gathered and used in the fields.

GÖREME (Maccan/Avcılar)

Göreme, situated 10km from Nevşehir, is found in the area surrounded with valleys, within the Nevşehir-Ürgüp-Avanos triangle. Old names for Göreme are Korama, Matiana, Maccan and Avcılar. Since Göreme was referred to as Korama in the earliest written document known from the 6th century, it is thought that it is the oldest name given to the community. In that document, it is said that St Hieron was born in Korama at the end of the 3rd century, was martyred in Melitene (modern Malatya) with his 30 friends and his hand was cut off and sent to his mother in Korama. A very large depiction of St Hieron of Korama is found in the Tokalı (Buckle) Church in the Göreme Open Air Museum. It is believed that Göreme and its surroundings were used as a necropolis by the people of Vanessa (Avanos) during the Roman Periods. Both the monumental twin pillared Roman tomb hollowed out of a fairy chimney in the centre of Göreme and the presence of numerous tombs in the vicinity support that idea.

Göreme, an important Christian centre in the early years of the Middle Ages, was a bishopric administered by Mokissos near Aksaray in the 11th and 13th centuries.

Despite the vast number of monasteries, churches and chapels in the vicinity of Göreme, there are not many inscriptions bearing dates. For this reason, these religious buildings are mainly dated according to their iconography or architectural features.

THE MOST FREQUENTLY FEATURED SCENES IN CAPPADOCIA'S CHURCHES

Deesis

One of the most frequently painted scenes in Cappadocia represents "Deesis", an old form of prayer. Jesus is pictured with Mary on his right and John the Baptist on his left, pleading for the souls of mankind. This scene is usually found on the main apse.

The Annunciation

In another scene, the Angel Gabriel visits the Virgin Mary, who is engaged to Joseph, and tells her that she will become pregnant by the Holy Spirit and give birth to a son called Jesus. In the miracle scene in Cappadocia's churches, Mary is usually pictured in front of her house talking to the angel.

The Visitation

After the incarnation Mary sets off on the road to Judea and greets Elizabeth and her husband Zacharias. Despite her age, her relative Elizabeth is also 6 months pregnant and bearing a son (Luke 1:26-27) As soon as Elizabeth hears Mary's greeting, her child leaps in her womb and she is filled with the Holy Spirit. She says, "Blessed are you among women, and blessed is the fruit of your womb!". (Luke, 1:39 - 56) In the picture showing this scene Mary is younger than Elizabeth and usually the two women are shown in an embrace.

The Journey to Bethlehem

During the reign of Caesar Augustus, he ordered a census of the population. Everyone had to go to their own town to register. For this reason Mary and Joseph set off from Nazareth to Bethlehem, the home of their ancestors. In this scene Mary is shown on an ass, Joseph and a manservant are also pictured making the journey.

The Nativity

On reaching Bethlehem, Mary and Joseph find all the inns full and are therefore obliged to stay in a stable. While in the stable Mary gives birth to a son. (Matthew 1:18-24; Luke 2:1- 7). In the birth scene Joseph, Mary and the baby Jesus are pictured in the stable. The baby Jesus is in a manger, behind which stand an ox and an ass warming Jesus with their breath. Mary is lying down and Joseph is looking surprised and deep in thought.

Adoration of the Magi (Wise Men)

The three wise men, Gaspar, Melchior and Balthazar see the star of Jesus in the East. They follow the star until they arrive at his birthplace. When they see Jesus they worship him and give him gifts of gold, frankincense and myrrh. (Matthew 2:1-12). In this scene one of the wise men is young, one is middle aged and the other, old. Their clothes resemble those of kings, which is why the scene is also called "The Adoration of the Kings".

Flight Into Egypt

After the departure of the wise men, an angel appears to Joseph in his dream. He tells him that King Herod intends to kill Jesus and he must therefore flee to Egypt with Mary and Jesus and wait there for a second message. At this time Herod issues an order that all children up to the age of two, in and around Bethlehem must be killed and the army is sent to carry out the order. When Herod dies, another angel appears to Joseph and tells him to take Mary and Jesus back to their own country. (Matthew 2: 13-18) In this scene Mary and the baby Jesus are riding on an ass and Joseph is following behind. A manservant is also pictured beside the family.

The Baptism

Jesus goes to the River Jordan, where John the Baptist is preaching and asks him to be baptized. John tries to deter Jesus saying, "I need to be baptized by you". Jesus replied, "Let it be so now; it is proper for us to do this to fulfill all righteousness" and John consented to baptize him. As soon as he is baptized Jesus emerges from the water and the skies open. The Holy Spirit in the form of a dove, descends and lands on Jesus, and a voice from heaven says, "This is my Son, whom I love; with him I am well pleased". (Matthew 4: 13-16; Mark 1:9-11; Luke 3: 21-22) In this scene Jesus is shown standing naked in the middle of the river. John has his hand on Jesus's head and two angels, placed on either side of Jesus, are holding a towel. In some pictures the devil can be seen clouding the river.

Göreme-1844 Texier

FIRST TRAVELLERS IN CAPPADOCIA

The Cappadocia region, in which many diverse civilizations lived was discovered by the Europeans at the beginning of the 18th century.

In 1744, Paul Lucas who was commissioned by Louis XIV, king of France, had declared that he had seen pyramid-like formed strange houses near Halys that had charming doors, stairs and large windows to illuminate the rooms. The fairy chimneys reminded him with the help of his imagination, of hooded priests and the rocks over them resembled the Virgin Mary holding the baby Christ, with the help of his imagination. In 1719, when Lucas resumed research in Cappadocia he defined these fairy chimneys as the graveyards that belong to Caesarea (modern Kayseri).

Lucas's fantastic description was reacted to with both suspicion and interest in the West.

C. Texier, who travelled in Cappadocia between 1833 - 1837 after Paul Lucas, stated that "nature had never showed itself to a foreigner's eyes so extraordinarily".

The English traveler Ainsworth who arrived in Cappadocia in 1837 described his impression with these words "Turning up a glen which led from the river inland, we found ourselves suddenly lost in a forest of cones and pillars of rock that rose around us in interminable confusion, like the ruins of some great and ancient city. At times, these rude pinnacles of rock balanced huge unformed masses upon their pointed summits but still more frequently the same strangely supported masses assumed fantastic shapes and forms. At one moment, it suggests the idea of a lion and at another of a bird and again of a crocodile or a fish."

Scientific researches and publications started toward the end of the 19th century.

The French researcher/priest G. De Jerphanion, who made observations for the French Union of Churches in 1907-1912, investigated the memorial rock churches, monasteries and the wall painting in them systematically.

Ürgüp/Texier-1844

Ürgüp/Texier-1844

CHURCHES AROUND GÖREME

El Nazar Church

This church is situated in the El Nazar valley, about 800m to the right from the road to the Göreme Open Air Museum. This church was carved from one piece of rock in a "T" shape. It is cruciform with three apses, the main apse opening up in the center where the barrel vaulted arms of the cruciform meet. The floor has been completely destroyed, as has part of the apse. The frescoes show scenes which follow each other in chronological order. This church can be dated to the end of the 10th century.

Scenes: Annunciation, Visitation, Nativity, Adoration of the Magi, Flight into Egypt, Presentation of Jesus in the Temple, Pursuit of Elizabeth, Baptism, Raising of Lazarus, Transfiguration, Entry into Jerusalem, Crucifixion, Anastasis, Ascension, and portraits of the saints.

Saklı (Hidden) Church

As this church remained undiscovered until 1957 it was given the name of Saklı, which means hidden. It is situated near the El Nazar Church. It is based on a broad rectangular plan, the main section being divided into two by two columns and three arches. It has three apses. The flat ceiling is decorated with crosses and geometrical patterns.

The frescoes in this church are painted directly onto the rock, and not onto plaster. Pieces of painted cloth found around the church have been analysed and found to be cloth which was used instead of brushes to paint the church. The architecture of the church resembles the style found in Mesopotamia. This church dates from the second half of the 11th century.

Scenes: Deesis, Annunciation, Nativity, Presentation of Jesus in the Temple, Calling of John, Baptism, Transfiguration, Crucifixion, Koimesis (Falling Asleep of St Mary the Virgin) and portraits of the saints.

Virgin Mary Church/Göreme

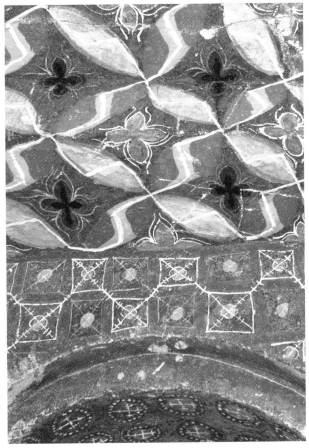

Virgin Mary Church/Göreme

Kılıçlar Kuşluk Church (of Mother Mary)

This church lies on a steep slope to the south of the Kılıçlar Church, and behind the Tokalı (Buckle) church, about 250m from the Open Air Museum. Two-barrel vaults of different widths and heights cover the rectangular nave. The church houses portraits of the saints, and four bible scenes.

Scenes: Deesis, Journey of Bethlehem, Nativity, Crucifixion, Koimesis (Falling Asleep of St Mary the Virgin) and the portraits of the saints.

Saklı (Hidden) ,Church

31

Kılıçlar Church

This church is situated 600m NW of the Göreme Open Air Museum in the Kılıçlar valley. It has a cruciform plan with four columns and a central dome. The arms of the cross are barrel vaulted. The ceilings in the West corners are flat, whereas those in the East corners are domed. There are three apses.

The walls are richly decorated with frescoes illustrating a long narration from the Bible. The church dates back to the end of the 9th and the beginning of the 10th centuries.

Scenes: Prophetic Vision, Annunciation, Visitation, Proof of the Virgin, Reproaches of Joseph, Nativity, Adoration of the Magi, Joseph's Dream, Flight into Egypt, Presentation of Jesus in the Temple, Calling of St. John the Baptist, John meeting Christ, Baptism, Jesus and Zacchaeus, Healing of the Blind Man, Raising of Lazarus, Entry into Jerusalem, Last Supper, Washing of the Disciples' Feet, Communion of the Disciples, Betrayal, Jesus before Annas and Caiaphas (chief Jewish priest), Jesus before Pilate, Denial by Peter, Way of the Cross, Crucifixion, Descent from the Cross, Entombment, Anastasis, Women at the Tomb, Blessing and Mission of the Apostles, Ascension, Pentecost, Koimesis (Falling Asleep of St Mary the Virgin) and portraits of the saints.

THE GÖREME OPEN AIR MUSEUM

By the end of the 2nd century a large Christian community had formed in Cappadocia. It is known that there were two bishoprics at that time; one in Kayseri, which, for a long time, continued to be a Christian center in the region and the other in Malatya. In the 3rd century, priests with good character changed the region into a lively centre of Christian activity.

In the 4th century Cappadocia became known as the land of the three saints; The Great St. Basil, Bishop of Kayseri; his brother St. Gregory of Nyssa, and St. Gregory of Nazianus. These three men created a new unity in Christian thought, and many of St. Basil's thoughts and actions are still important today.

An example of his doctrine is the advice to Christian with one piece of bread in a famine. He said that a Christian should give half of his bread to a fellow believer and trust in God to take care of him.

St. Basil founded small, secluded settlements far away from villages and towns. Daily worship was carried out under the supervision of a preacher.

These groups were not, however, privileged groups separated from the community like similar communities in Egypt and Syria. St. Basil is important in that he introduced worship within the community in the churches of Cappadocia. Göreme Open Air Museum is the place where this kind of religious education was started. The same model was then introduced in Soğanlı, Ihlara and Açıksaray.

Church Architecture in Göreme

The one nave barrel vaulted plan common for Göreme's churches was the most convenient architectural style for the religious communities and those living in seclusion in the area. These buildings were also seen as suitable areas for graves. The transversal rectangular plan originated in Mesopotamia, and it is likely that these buildings were constructed for groups of foreigners settling in the area. In Göreme, the only church built with two naves is the church of St. Eustathios, however, the churches in Soğanlı and Ihlara quite often feature two naves. Buildings according to the basilica plan with three naves are also rare in Göreme, this being a preferred technique for the Bishopric churches such as Durmuş Kadir. These churches were big and the architecture was very ornate, and for this reason this style was not popular in rocky areas.

Tokalı (Buckle) Church

This is the oldest known rock-cut church in the region, and is comprised of four sections: The Old Church with one nave; the New Church; the Lower Church under the Old Church; and the Parecclesion to the north of the New Church. The single-naved, barrel-vaulted Old Church, built in the 10th century, today acts as the entrance to the New Church.

Its apse collapsed when the New Church was added to the east wing. Frescoes are to be found on the vault and at the top of the walls. The life of Jesus is told on separate panels on the vault, running from left to right.

Scenes: Portraits of the saints are in the center of the vault. On the top panel of the right wing are Annunciation, Visitation, Proof of the Virgin, Journey to Bethlehem, and Nativity. On the top panel of the left wing are, Adoration of the Magi, Massacre of the Innocents, Flight into Egypt, Presentation of Jesus in the Temple and Killing of Zacharias. On the middle panel of the right wing are, Pursuit of Elizabeth, Calling of St. John the Baptist, Preaching of John, John meeting Jesus, Baptism and Marriage at Cana. On the middle panel of the left wing are, Miracle of the Wine, Miracle of the Loaves and Fishes, Calling of the Disciples, Healing of the Blind Man and Raising of Lazarus. On the lower panel of the right wing is Entry into Jerusalem, Last supper, Betrayal and Jesus before Pilate. On the left lower panel of the left wing are Way of the Cross, Crucifixion, Descent from the Cross, Entombment, Women at the Tomb, Anastasis and Ascension. Beneath this panel are portraits of the saints. The Transfiguration is painted over the entrance.

Visitation, Proof of the Virgin, Journey to Bethlehem/Old Tokalı Church

Virgin Mary and Jesus/New Tokalı Church

ΑΠΕΤΡΟΣ ΕΧΟΡΙΣΕΝ ΤΟCΕΥ ΤΑ ΔΙΑΚΟΝΑ CΕΙ
ΤΟΝ ΕΥΔΟΜΙ ΚΟΝΤΑ ΑΠΟCΤΟΛΟ ΝΙC
ΠΕΘΙΚΝΕΠΑΤΟΥCΤΑC ΧΙΡΑΙCΗΤΑΟΗ C
ΥΤΩ

ΙΑΘΗΤΑCΟΙΝΙCC ΕΝΟΙ

The New Church is transversally rectangular with a simple barrel vault. On the east wall there are four columns joined by arches, behind which there is a raised corridor in front of the main apse and two side apses. On this barrel vaulted nave is the story of Jesus in chronological order in mainly bright red and blue colors. The dark blue color serves to distinguish the Tokalı Church from the other churches.

On the transversal nave are scenes from the life of St. Basil, portraits of some saints and pictures of the Miracles of Jesus. The Church is dated back to last decade of the 10th century and the first decade of the 11th century. Scenes: On the north wing of the vault are Annunciation, Visitation, Proof of the Virgin, Nativity and Adoration of the Magi.

On the north wall of the vault are Joseph's Dream and Journey to Bethlehem and below these in the niches are portraits of 8 saints. At the very bottom are Calling of St. John the Baptist, John meeting Jesus, Baptism, Presentation of Jesus in the Temple, Calling of Matthew, Calling of the Disciples and Marriage at Cana; on the west wing Flight into Egypt,

Temptation of Christ and Christ in the Temple when Twelve Years Old, on the south wing of the vault are the First Diacons, Pentecost and Blessing and Mission of the Apostles; on the south wall of the vault are some unidentified angels, below them, in the niches, are portraits of saints; at the very bottom are Healing of the Nobleman's Son, Raising the Daughter of Jairus, Healing the Paralytic, Raising of Lazarus, Entry into Jerusalem and Last Supper. On the west wing is Washing of the Disciples' Feet, on the main apse conch are the Crucifixion, Descent from the Cross, Women at the Tomb, Anastasis. On the front wall of the apse are the First Diacons and Jesus and the Samaritan Woman; inside the niche is Mother Mary and baby Jesus; and on the apse to the north is the Prophetic Vision and angels.

New Tokalı Church

Crucifixion/New Tokalı Church

Calling of the Apostles /New Tokalı Church

Nunnery and Monastery

The 6-7 storey rock mass to the left of the museum entrance is known as the "Nunnery". The dining hall, kitchen and some rooms on the first floor, together with the ruined chapel on the second level, can still be visited. The church on the third storey, which can be reached through a tunnel, has a cruciform plan, a dome with four columns and three apses. The templon on the main apse is rarely found in Göreme's churches. Besides the fresco of Jesus, painted directly onto the rock, designs painted in red can also be seen. The different levels of the monastery are connected by tunnels, and "millstone doors", such as those found in the underground cities, which were used to close off these tunnels in times of danger. The tunnels connecting the levels of the Monastery, to the right, have eroded making it possible to only visit some of the ground floor rooms.

Chapel of St. Basil

This church is situated at the entrance to the Göreme Open Air Museum. Graves are to be found in the columned narthex area. The nave is transversally rectangular and barrel vaulted, and has three apses situated on the left, long side of the rectangular nave. The church dates back to the 11th century.

Scenes: On the main apse is a portrait of Jesus, and next to this is a portrait of Mary and Baby Jesus. On the north wall is picture of St. Theodore, while St. George and the dragon are featured on the south wall. The paintings of St Demetrius and two female saints can also be seen.

Elmalı (Apple) Church

This church featuring four columns, nine domes and three apses is of the closed cruciform type. Access to the church is through a tunnel on the north side. The original entrance was on the west side. The original decorations in this church consist of geometrical designs and crosses painted in red ochre directly onto the rock. This technique is also found in the chapels of St. Barbara and St. Basil. The church has been dated back to the mid 11th century and the beginning of the 12th century.

Scenes: Deesis, Nativity, Adoration of the Magi, Baptism, Raising of Lazarus, Transfiguration, Entry into Jerusalem, Last Supper, Betrayal of Judas, Way of the Cross, Crucifixion, Entombment, Anastasis, Women at the Tomb, Ascension and portraits of the saints. There are also scenes from the Old Testament such as the Hospitality of Abraham and Three Young Men in the Fiery Furnace.

Elmalı Church

Chapel of St. Barbara

This church is situated behind the rock housing the Elmalı (Apple) Church. It has a cruciform plan, with two columns. The north, south and west arms of the cruciform are barrel vaulted, and the centre, the east arm, and the east corners are domed.

There are a main, central apse and two side apses. Motifs were painted in red directly onto the rock. The walls and the dome are decorated in a variety of motifs including geometrical patterns, mythological animals and military symbols. The walls also have motifs resembling stonework. This church dates back to the second half of the 11th century.

Scenes: On the main apse is Christ Pantocrator, on the north arm are St.George and the Dragon and St Theodore, and on the west arm is St Barbara.

Yılanlı (Snake) Church (of St. Onuphorius)

The main section is transversally rectangular and barrel vaulted, whereas the extended space to the south, which houses the graves, has a flat ceiling. The apse was hollowed out of the long wall on the left and the church was left uncompleted. The entrance to the church is from the north. Portraits of the respected saints of Cappadocia are on either side of the vault. The church dates back to the 11th century.

Scenes: Opposite the entrance is a portrait of Jesus holding the Bible in his left hand. The donor of the church is pictured beside Jesus. On the east side of the vault are St. Onesimus, St. George and the Dragon, St.Theodore, and Helena holding the True Cross with her son Constantine the Great. On the west of the vault is the longhaired, naked St. Onuphoius behind a palm tree, with St. Thomas in a sanctifying position beside him, and St. Basil holding a book.

In the first century AD people calling themselves "Hermits" lived in seclusion in the Egyptian deserts. They dedicated themselves to religion. In the 4th century, St. Paphnutius traveled to Egypt to learn about the hermits' way of life, and there he met St. Onuphrius, whom the church was named after. St. Paphnutius helped St. Onuphrius while he was dying, as he was the best example of moral values and self control. St. Onuphrius is depicted as naked, longhaired and broad chested, and a palm tree is in front of him.

St.George and St. Theodore/Yılanlı Church

Larder/Kitchen/Refectory

These three areas lie side by side and are connected by passageways. The first section was used as a larder, with recesses hollowed from the rock being used as storage spaces.

In the kitchen there is a "tandir", a type of oven still found in local village houses. The final section was the refectory. A long table carved from the rock extends from the left of the entrance. This would have seated 40-50 people. To the right of the table is a winery hollowed in the floor used for squashing grapes.

Karanlık (Dark) Church

To the north, a winding stairway leads into the rectangular, barrel vaulted narthex of the Dark Church. This church has a cruciform plan, the arms of which are cross-vaulted. There is a center dome, with four columns and three apses. This church gets its name from the tiny window in the narthex which only allows a small amount of light in. Due to the absence of light the colors of the frescoes are still vivid.

The church and the narthex are richly decorated in scenes from the Bible and the story of Jesus. As in Elmalı (Apple) and Çarıklı churches, there are also scenes from the Old Testament. The church dates back to the end of the 12th and beginning of the 13th centuries.

Scenes: Deesis, Annunciation, Journey to Bethlehem, Nativity, Adoration of the Magi, Baptism, Raising of Lazarus, Transfiguration, Entry into Jerusalem, Last Supper, Betrayal of Judas, Crucifixion, Anastasis, Women at the Tomb, Blessing and Mission of the Apostles, Ascension, Hospitality of Abraham, Three Young Men in the Fiery Furnace and portraits of the saints.

Anastasis/Karanlık Church

Betrayal of Judas/Karanlık Church

Last Supper/Karanlık Church

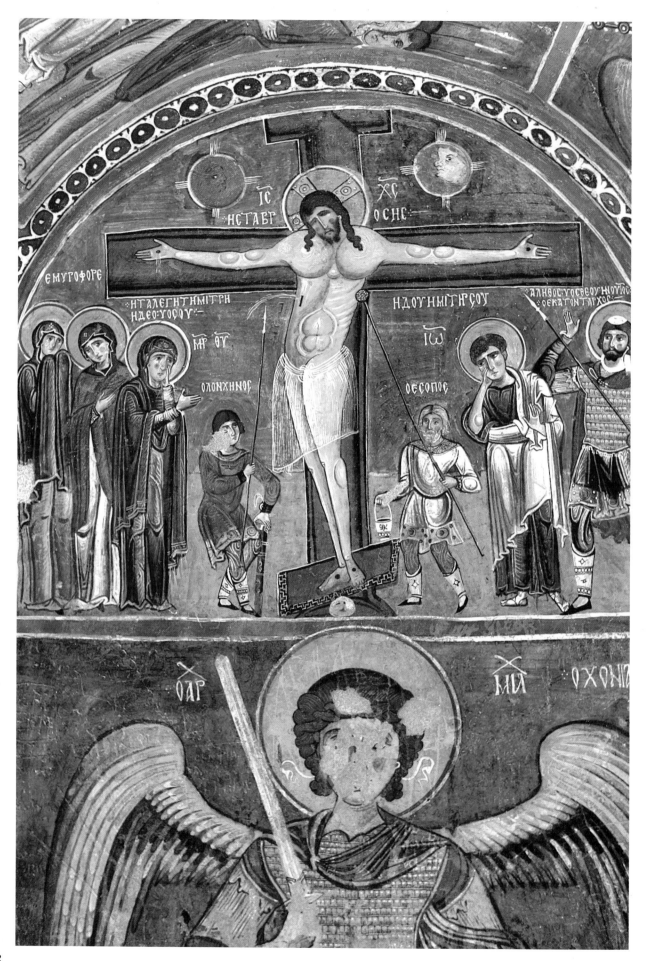

Chapel of St Catherine

Situated between the Karanlık (Dark) Church and the Çarıklı Church, the Chapel of St. Catherine has a free-cross nave and narthex. The central bay is covered by a dome and the cross arms are barrel- vaulted. Its apse is closed by a templon. The narthex has nine floor graves and two arcosolia (burial niches). Only in the nave of the chapel are some decorations with figures. The pendentives are decorated with carvings. The Chapel of St. Catherine, built by a donor named Anna, dates back to the 11th century. Scenes: Deesis in the apse with the templon, below are Doctors of the Church (Gregory, Basil the Great and John Chrysostom), on the south wall of the northern arm is St. George, opposite St. Theodore, St. Catherine and other panels of saints.

Crucifixion/Karanlık Church

Çarıklı (Sandals) Church

This two columned church (two other columns being in the form of pillars), is cross vaulted, and has three apses and four domes. The well preserved frescoes show the life of Jesus, Hospitality of Abraham, and images of the saints and the donors of the church. Although it resembles the Karanlık (Dark) and Elmalı (Apple) Churches, the scenes of Way of the Cross and Descent from the Cross make this church different from the others. The figures are generally large. The footprints under the Ascension scene give the church its name, which means "with sandal". The church dates back to the end of the 12th and the beginning of the 13th centuries. The center dome houses a picture of Jesus the Pantocrator with the busts of angels in the insets. On the central apse is Deesis, on the north apse Mary and the Baby Jesus, and on the south apse, a picture of St Michael. Scenes: Nativity, Adoration of the Magi, Baptism, Raising of Lazarus, Transfiguration, Entry into Jerusalem, Betrayal, Women at the Tomb, Anastasis, Ascension and portraits of the saints.

Shepherds/Çarıklı Church

49

Blessing and Mission of the Apostles/Çavuşin Church

ÇAVUŞİN

One of the oldest settlements in the area, Çavuşin is situated 2km from Göreme, on the Göreme - Avanos road. The Church of St. John the Baptist offers a panoramic view of the village. This church and its paintings date back to the 5th century, making it the oldest church in the region.

It had a large courtyard which is unusual for Cappadocia, This has eroded away however. Christian missionaries and communities once lived in the old Çavuşin valley, now in ruins. There are 5 churches at Güllüdere, close to Çavuşin. The Haçlı Church (with the Cross), near the valley, was also used for defence against the Arab raiders.

Çavuşin (Nicephorus Phocas) Church

This barrel vaulted church, with one nave and three apses, is situated 2.5km from Göreme on the Göreme-Avanos road. Its narthex is collapsed. The church was built around 964/965AD.

Scenes: On the vault are Annunciation, Visitation, Proof of the Virgin, Flight into Egypt, Joseph's Dream II, Blessing and Mission of the Apostles, Adoration of the Magi, Massacre of the Innocents, Pursuit of Elizabeth, and Killing of Zacharias. On the west wall are Joseph and Mary After Proving, Journey to Bethlehem, Nativity, Last Supper, Betrayal of Judas, Anastasis, Baptism. On the north wall are Jesus before Pilate, Way of the Cross, Crucifixion, and Death of Christ, and on the south wall are Entry into Jerusalem, Raising of Lazarus, Healing of the Blind Man, Descent from the Cross, and Women at the Tomb. On the wall of the apse is the Transfiguration, and on the north apse Emperor Nicephorus Phocas and his family. He held power and authority in Cappadocia at that time.

Çavuşin

Marble sarcophagus from Avanos-Nevşehir Museum

AVANOS (Venessa)

The ancient name of the town of Avanos, which lies 18km to the northeast of Nevsehir, is Vanessa. The main economic activity in the town is pottery, a craft dating back to the Hittite period. The red clay which is worked by local craftsmen comes from the residue in the Kızılırmak river. On the banks of the Kızılırmak, near to Avanos, a marble sarcophagus was found in a Roman necropolis. It is particularly interesting as it is the first sarcophagus to have been found in the area. The sarcophagus was discovered in 1971, but unfortunately someone had already opened the gable roof lid and stolen the contents.

After pathological and paleoanthropological tests on the the body and sarcophagus it has been established that the body belonged to a woman, whose hair was dyed with henna. The 13th century Sarihan Caravansary and the Ottoman Alaaddin mosque are interesting pieces of architecture in the area.

ZELVE

Zelve is situated on the northern slopes of Aktepe, 1km from Paşabağları (Monks' Valley) and 5 km from Avanos. The ruins at Zelve are spread over three valleys, which also house several pointed fairy chimneys with large stems. The valley was inhabited until 1952.

Besides monasteries and churches, houses, a tunnel joining two of the valleys, a mill, a mosque and several dove-cotes are found in the valley. Like the ones in Uçhisar, Göreme and Çavuşin, it is not known when the rock dwellings in Zelve were first inhabited but it was an important settlement and religious area during the 9th and 13th centuries. The first seminaries for priests were established here.

The Direkli Church (with Columns), situated at the bottom of the slopes, dates back to the early years of monastery life in Zelve. The main decorations are high relief crosses representative of the Iconoclastic doctrine. Some of the most important churches in the valley are Balıklı (Fish), Üzümlü (Grape) and Geyikli (Deer), all belonging to the Pre-Iconoclastic period.

Balıklı (Fish) and Üzümlü (Grape) Churches

The churches are situated to the east of a monastery courtyard, in the third valley in Zelve. Above the entrance to the Fish and the Grape Churches, which has partly collapsed, is the depiction of the Enthroned Mother Mary holding the Baby Jesus.

On the partly collapsed vault are Archangels Gabriel and Michael holding up a Maltese Cross. To the right of the entrance is the single naved, barrel vaulted cell-like "South Chapel" with an apse. Inside the chapel, on the sides, there are seating platforms.

On the apse, in a red frame, is pictured Jesus standing and holding a book in one hand and blessing with the other. The front of the apse is decorated with series of simple triangles and circles with dots in them and the vault is decorated with a Maltese Cross and concentric circles. The chapel probably dates back to the 10th century.

Second and Third Valley/Zelve

Grape Church/Zelve

Third Valley/Zelve

Mill/Zelve

Paşabağları (Monks' Valley) and St. Simeon Dwelling

Formerly known as the "Monks' Valley" (Rahipler Valley), Paşabağları is situated about 1 km from the Göreme-Avanos road. Many fairy chimneys with multiple stems and caps, some housing chapels and living areas can be found here, This style is unique to this area. A chapel dedicated to St. Simeon, and a hermit's shelter are built into one such fairy chimney with three tops. The entrance of the cell, which can be reached through a chimney like narrow tunnel, that is decorated with antithetical crosses.

St. Simeon was living in seclusion near Aleppo in Syria during the 5th century, and rumours began spreading that he worked miracles. Disturbed by all the attention, he began to live at the top of a 2m high column, and later moved to one 15m in height. From there he only descended occasionally to get the food and drink brought by his disciples.

The hermits of Cappadocia distanced themselves from the world by cutting into fairy chimneys rather than living on top of columns. They hollowed out the chimneys from top to bottom creating rooms 10-15m high. They lay on beds made from rock, fed by locals via buckets that were lifted by ropes to their lofty perches.

St. Simeon dwelling

Paşabağları

Paşabağları

ÜRGÜP

One of the most important centers in Cappadocia is Ürgüp, 20km to the east of Nevşehir. Like Göreme, Ürgüp also had different names in history; Osiana (Assiana) in the Byzantine Period, Başhisar during the Seljuk Peroid, Burgut Castle in the Ottoman Period and Ürgüp during the early years of the Republic. The earliest known settlement in the area was on the outskirts of Mount Avla, to the north of the Damsa river which was refered to as "Tomissos" in antiquity. The most important remains belonging to the later period are the Roman tombs found in the towns and villages near Ürgüp.

Also an important religious center during the Byzantine Period, Ürgüp was a bishopric of the rock-cut churches and monasteries found in the villages, towns and valleys around Ürgüp. In the 11th century, Ürgüp was an important citadel connecting with Niğde and Konya, important towns of Seljuks. The two buildings from this period are the Altıkapılı (Six Gates) and Temenni Tepesi (Wish Hill) tombs found in the town center.

The 13th century Altıkapılı tomb, housing the remains of a mother and her two daughters, has six sides each with an arched window and no roof.

Although researchers think that this is unlikely, one of the two tombs on the Temenni Hill is believed to belong to Seljuk Sultan Rüknettin Kılıçarslan IV, built by Vecihi Pasha in 1268 and is known as "Kılıçarslan Tomb" by the locals.

The other one is believed to belong to Alaaddin Keykubat III. Ürgüp became a part of the Ottoman Empire in 1515. It was the first time in the 18th century when Damat Ibrahim Pasha, the Ottoman Grand Vezier, established the governorship in Nevşehir (Muskara). Ürgüp was then administered by the governorship making Ürgüp secondary in importance. In his history and geography book "Kamus-ül Alam" written between 1888 and 1890, Semseddin Sami mentions 70 mosques, 5 churches and 11 libraries in Ürgüp.

Devrent Valley

ORTAHİSAR

Ortahisar citadel, built both as a defense and as a settlement, is situated 6km from Ürgüp, on the road to Nevşehir. Typical examples of the area's civilian architecture can be found among the houses skirting the citadel. The sides of the valleys are littered with carved out storage areas used for preserving local products such as apples and potatoes, as well as oranges and lemons brought from the Mediterranean. Very interesting churches and monasteries can be found in the surrounding valleys. Among these are, Sarıca Church, Cambazlı Church, Tavşanlı Church, Balkan Deresi Churches and Hallaç Dere Monastery.

Üzümlü (Grape) Church

The Grape Church is located at the beginning of the Red Valley, to the west of the town of Ortahisar, about 1 km from the road. The fairy chimney, in which the Grape Church is found, is hollowed out like a monastic complex, where monks lived.

The lower level of the fairy chimney is the church and the upper level is a chamber which can be seen only from the outside due to the partial collapse of the walls. There is a cross relief on the ceiling. The church has a square plan with one apse and one nave. At the far end of the nave is a grave niche. This church is also called The Church of St. Nichitas due to the presence of an inscription of St Nichitas in the dedication inscription of the church.

The nave with a flat ceiling is decorated with rich embellishments. The orange colored surface is decorated with a cross composed of circles and rectangles and bunches of grape and geometrical motifs around it. The border is embellished using medallions with Maltese crosses. Although it is not definite, the common belief is that the church dates back to the 8th or 9th century.

Scenes: On the apse Enthroned Mary holding Baby Jesus and Archangels Michael and Gabriel by their sides, on the north and south sides of the nave twelve apostles and doctor saints.

Kızılçukur\Ortahisar

Üzümlü Church/Kızılçukur

Üzümlü Church/Kızılçukur

63

MUSTAFAPAŞA (Sinasos)

Mustafapaşa, 6km to the south of Ürgüp, was inhabited by Greek Orthodox families until the beginning of the 20th century. The houses dating back to the end of the 19th and beginning of the 20th centuries display fine examples of stonework. The Gömede valley, to the west of Mustafapaşa, resembles a small version of the Ihlara valley. As at Ihlara, the walls of the valley house churches and shelters carved from the rock, and a river runs through the valley.

The important churches and monasteries around Mustafapaşa are, the church of Aios Vasilos, the Church of Constantine-Helene, churches in the Monastery Valley and, the Church of St. Basil in the Gömede valley. There is also a medresse built during the Ottoman period and displaying fine examples of stone masonry and woodcraft

Şakir Mehmet Paşa Medresse/Mustafapaşa

Aios Vasilios Church/Mustafapaşa

TATLARİN

The village of Tatlarin, located 10 km north of the town of Acıgöl, is one of the most interesting places in Cappadocia because of both its underground settlement and churches and the architecture of its houses. Its underground settlement, located on the hill called "the castle" by the locals of the village, was first discovered in 1975 and opened to the public in 1991. The size of the chambers in the underground settlement, only two floors of which can be visited; the presence of the toilets, which also can only be found at the Guzelyurt Underground Settlement; the abundance of the depots for food and of the churches make one think that this place was either a garrison or a monastic complex rather than an underground settlement.

Tatlarin Church

The church is on the slope of the hill, called "the castle", in the town of Tatlarin, 10km north of Acıgöl. The narthex of the church, which has two naves and two apses, is collapsed. The well preserved scenes are separated from each other with dividers. The background is dark grey whereas colours like purple, mustard color and red are used for the figures.

Scenes: On the apse Mother Mary and Baby Jesus, Archangels Michael and Gabriel; Constantine the Great and Helena, Transfiguration, Anastasis, Entry into Jerusalem, Crucifixion and portraits of 9 saints as well as one of the donor.

Anastasis/Tatlarin Church

NEVŞEHİR

Nevşehir's ancient name was "Nyssa", but in the Ottoman period it was renamed "Muşkara". The son in law of Sultan Ahmet III, the Ottoman Grand Vizier Ibrahim Pasa was born in Nevşehir and therefore took a great interest in its construction. The small village originally had only 18 houses. Once it came under the administration of Ürgüp, was transformed with the building of mosques, fountains, schools, soup kitchens, inns and bath houses, and its name was changed from Muşkara to Nevşehir, which means New City.

Damat İbrahim Paşa Complex

Kurşunlu mosque, situated in the Damat İbrahim Paşa complex, was completed in 1726. The mosque which is situated in the centre of a court with three gates, has an elegant minaret 44 m in height. The name "Kurşunlu" comes from the sheets of lead covering the main dome. Most of the internal decorations consist of floral motifs.

A Medrese (College of Islamic theology), library, soup kitchen and a bath house are contained in the same complex. The citadel found on the highest point of the city was constructed in the Selcuk Period to defend and protect the caravan trails.

GÜLŞEHIR

The old name of Gülşehir, situated on the southern bank of the Red River, 20 km from Nevşehir, is Arapsun and in ancient times it was called "Zoropassos". The Ottoman Grand Vezier Karavezir Mehmet Seyyid Pasha did the same thing in Gülşehir as Damat Ibrahim Pasha did in Nevşehir and a külliye was built in the town which had only 30 houses. The complex consisted of a mosque, a medresse and a fountain.

Açıksaray Ruins

This important area of ruins is situated 3 km from Gülşehir. There are numerous rock cuttings including Roman tombs, and churches dating back to the 9th and 11th centuries in this important bishopric.

The mihrab in "the Mescid of Hacı Bektaş-i Veli", as it is called by locals, is interesting as it is a well preserved Islamic building. To the west side of the mescid, with a square-like plan, are some quite large niches. Rock formations in the shape of mushrooms are unique to this area.

Last Judgement/St. Jean Church

Karşı Church (of St John)

The two floor church of St. John, found on entering Gülşehir, houses a church, wine cellar, graves, water channels and living quarters on the lower floor, and a church decorated with biblical scenes on the upper floor.

The lower floor church is built to the shape of a cross, has one apse and arms of the cross are barrel-vaulted. The central dome is collapsed. Stylized animals, geometrical and crucifix designs in red ochre are used to decorate the church, which was applied directly onto the rock.

The upper church has one apse, and is barrel-vaulted. Apart from those on the apse, the well-preserved frescoes were covered in a layer of black soot. The church's present state owes to restoration and conservation done by Rıdvan İşler in 1995.

The scenes of Jesus and the Bible are in the form of friezes within the borders. Yellow and red colors have been used on a black background. On the niche vault and on the sides, floral and geometrical patterns were used. On the west and south walls the Last Judgement can be found, a scene rarely depicted in Cappadocian churches. According to the inscription on the apse, the church is dated to 1212.

Scenes: Deesis on the apse, on its front Annunciation, below bird designs, on the barrel vault portrait of Saints in medallions, on the south wing of the vault Last Supper, Betrayal by Judas, Baptism, below Koemesis, on the north wings of the vault Descent from the Cross, Women at the Tomb, Anastasis, on the west and south walls the Last Judgement.

Betrayal of Judas/ St. Jean Church

Last Judgement/St. Jean Church

71

HACIBEKTAŞ

This town gets its name from Hacı Bektaş-i Veli, who made an effort to unite Turkish customs and culture with the Islamic faith, and worked hard to protect the Turkish language and culture from foreign influence and degeneration. Born in the 13th century in Khorassan, bordering today's modern day Iran, Hacı Bektas was educated by Ahmet Yesevi, a learned thinker of that time.

Haci Bektaş migrated west and arrived in Anatolia, where he settled in Hacimköy near Sulucakarahöyük. His arrival coincided with the political and economic deterioration of the Anatolian Selcuk state, during which time the central authority collapsed. Hacı Bektaş travelled from city to city and from village to village to promote Turkish unity.

Early Bronze Age, Hittite, Phrygian, Hellenistic, and Roman artifacts unearthed during excavations carried out in the town's center are on display at the Archaeological Museum of Hacı Bektaş.

Hacı Bektaş-i Veli Museum

The Hacı Bektaş-i Veli Museum houses the tombs of Hacı Bektaş-i Veli and Balım Sultan, a mosque, bathhouse, kitchen, laundry, guest house, several fountains, and three courtyards.

Through a big arched door, one enters the first courtyard, Nadar;"Üçler Cesmesi," the Fountain of the Three, built in 1902, the bathhouse, and the laundry are in this courtyard.

The entrance to the second courtyard, Dergah, is called "Üçler Kapısı", the Gate of the Three. The Lion Fountain, built in 1554 was sent from Egypt by the daughter of Kavalalı Mehmet Ali Pasha in 1875. It is on display in this area. In addition, the guesthouse, soup kitchen, and mosque built during the time of Mahmut II, the Ottoman Sultan, are in Dergah.

The entrance to the third courtyard, Hazret, is called "Altılılar Kapısı", the Gate of the Six. This garden contains the tombs of dervishes, Horasan Erleri -the Khorassan Men-, Güvenç Abdal, Hacı Bektaş, and Balım Sultan, Hacı Bektaş's successor. Hacı Bektaş's tomb features Seljuk architecture and designs. The sarcophagus is covered with a green quilt and is adorned with ornamental candlesticks.

IHLARA VALLEY

This valley is fourteen kilometers long and ranging from 100 to150 meters high. Ihlara Valley stretches from Ihlara to Selime. Situated 40 kilometers from Aksaray, the canyon we see today was eroded by the Melendiz River, which found its way through cracks in the basalt and andesite lava, deposited by Mt. Hasandağ. Historically, the Melendiz River was called "Potamus Kapadukus," which means "River of Cappadocia."

This valley proved to be an ideal place for monks to worship in seclusion, as well as provide a safe hide-away and place of defense for people during times of invasion. There are numerous dwellings, churches, and graves built into the valley walls, some of which are connected by tunnels and corridors.

The decorations in the churches date from the 6th to the 13th centuries, and the churches can be classified into two groups.

The churches nearer to Ihlara display frescoes with oriental influence, and those nearer to Belisırma display Byzantine style decorations. The most well preserved frescoes are found in the churches of Ağaçaltı, Pürenliseki, Kokar, Yılanlı and Kırkdamaltı.

Although very few Byzantine inscriptions in this area can be read, the names of Seljuk Sultan Mesud II (1282-1305) and the Byzantine Emperor Andronicos II are inscribed above a 13th century fresco in the church of St. George (Kırkdamaltı). This is evidence of the tolerance of Seljuk rulers.

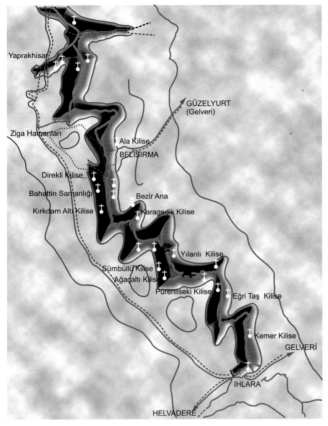

Ağaçaltı Church (Beneath the Tree)

This church, dated from the 9th-11th centuries, is known as the church of St. Daniel, due to the picture of Daniel on the wall opposite the entrance. The cruciform plan contains domes, a barrel vaulted ceiling, and three apses, two of which at the main entrance are collapsed. Red, grey, and yellow were used on a white background to decorate the church. The vault of the north arm of the cross is covered in various motifs.

Scenes: Annunciation, Visitation, Nativity, Adoration of the Magi, Flight into Egypt, Baptism of Jesus, Koimesis (Falling Asleep of Mother Mary), Daniel in the Lions' Den, the Ascension, and portraits of the saints.

Ascension/Ağaçaltı Church

Kokar Church

This 9th century church is entered by way of a collapsed apse and contains a burial area. Greyish colors dominate the paintings, including a large cross adorned with geometrical patterns, painted on the well-preserved vault. The picture of a hand giving the symbol of the Holy Trinity is painted in the center of a cross.

Scenes: Deesis, Annunciation, Visitation, Proof of the Virgin, Nativity, Adoration of the Magi, Baptism, Three Young Men in the Fiery Furnace, Flight into Egypt, Last Supper, Betrayal of Judas, Crucifixion, Women at the Tomb, Ascension, Entombment, Pentecost and portraits of saints.

Yılanlı (Snake) Church

This barrel-vaulted church has one apse and is built on a cruciform plan. Monks' graves are housed in the chapel on the north wall. The church gets its name from the painting of four naked, sinful women being attacked by serpents on the west wall.

As the inscriptions have been worn away, the sin of the first woman attacked by 8 serpents is unknown. The second woman's breast is being attacked because she did not breastfeed her child. The third woman's mouth is being attacked for telling lies, and the fourth's ears are under attack because she was disobedient. This church dates back to the end of the 9th century.

SELİME

Selime is situated at the end of the Ihlara Valley. Fairy chimneys rest on the steep hillside. A basilica style cathedral, a citadel, various churches, and the Seljuk tomb of Selime Sultan, for whom the town was named, are found here.

GÜZELYURT

Güzelyurt is 45km from Aksaray and 15km from Ihlara. Visitors to Cappadocia will appreciate the beautiful natural scenery accented by 19th century architecture. Gregory of Nazianzus, who was dedicated to spreading Christianity in the area, turned Güzelyurt into place of importance.

Yüksek, Kızıl, Silvişli, Ahmatlı and Koç are churches located in Güzelyurt. It also contains a church built in 1891, now used as a mosque.

Hasandağ

Selime

Eğri Minaret/Aksaray

AKSARAY

Aksaray is situated on a large plain at the base of Mt. Hasan. It gets its name from the Cappadocian king, Archelaos, and was an important town during the Roman period. The name was changed to Aksaray by the Seljuks in the 11th century.

Kızıl Minaret/Aksaray

Aksaray boasts the oldest piece of Seljuk work, the Eğri (Kızıl) Minaret, built between 1221-1236 by Sultan Keyhüsrev I, the father of the Seljuk Sultan Alaeddin Keykubat. It has a cubical pedestal and cylindered body. Its body is divided by a thin moulding. The lower part of the Eğri Minaret is decorated with zigzag designs, whereas the upper part is covered with blue and green tiles. Unfortunately, most of these tiles are missing. 92 stone steps lead to the minaret's balcony.

There is no definite record about when the minaret, called Turkey's Tower of Pisa, started to lean.

According to an inscription from the time of the Ottoman Sultan Murat IV, the real name of the red brick minaret is Keyhüsrev, however, it is known as Eğri (Inclined), or Kızıl (Red), by the locals. The province of Aksaray houses the 15th century Ulucami and the Medrese of Zinciriye, Ihlara Valley, and Güzelyurt.

Ulu Mosque/Aksaray

SOĞANLI VALLEY

This valley is situated near Yeşilhisar in the province of Kayseri, 40km southeast of Ürgüp, and 25km to the east of Derinkuyu. Fractures and collapses during earthquakes have added to erosion, resulting in deep valleys and canyons.

Soğanlı Valley, which is divided into two, has been occupied since the Roman period. The Romans used the conical rock formations as graves, and later, Byzantines transformed them into churches.

The frescoes in the church date back to the 9th and 13th centuries. Karabaş, Yılanlı, Kubbeli and the Church of St. Barbara (Tahtalı) are notable churches in the valley.

Karabaş Church

Found on the right side of the valley, this church has one nave, one apse, and a barrel-vaulted ceiling. The 11th century church was painted over an extended period of time, and exhibits various painting techniques. Scenes: Diesis, Annunciation, Nativity, Presentation of Jesus in the Temple, Transfiguration, Missions of the Apostles, Crucifixion, Anastasis, Ascension and portraits of saints. In addition to this church, graves, large vaulted chapels, and priests' rooms can be found among the rock mass.

Presentation of Jesus in the Temple/Karabaş Church

Soğanlı Valley

Anastasis/St. Barbara Church

Tahtalı Church (of St. Barbara)

This church lies at the end of the valley, to the west of the village. The barrel -vaulted church contains a single apse and as well as a single nave. The vault is divided with a projecting line. The church dates to the early 10th century and contains many portraits of the saints.

Scenes: Prophetic Vision, Diesis, Annunciation, Visitation, Proof of the Virgin, Journey to Bethlehem, Nativity, Anastasis, Seven Sleepers, and portraits of the saints.

Özlüce underground City

SUBTERREANEAN SETTLEMENTS OF CAPPADOCIA

One of the cultural highlights of the Cappadocia Region is the abundance of subterranean settlements commonly referred to as "underground cities." Because the region had been subjected to frequent raids, these cities were built to provide people with places where they could take temporary shelter during times of danger. Carved out of the soft tufa rock within a 25,000 square km region, the underground cities were connected to many houses, by way of hidden passages. To provide greater protection from enemies, the people laid traps in various places of the rock dwellings and strategically fashioned the entryways in hard-to-reach locations. When needed, new rooms were hollowed out under the floors of the existing rooms, increasing the size of the underground settlements.

There are 150-200 known underground and cliff settlements of varying sizes in the Cappadocia region, but due to the sheer size of the region, it is possible that not all have been discovered. A few underground cities were large enough to accommodate 30,000 people while other settlements could more accurately be described as "underground villages."

Structural Features

Long passages and labyrinth-like tunnels connect hundreds of rooms in the underground cities. Small hollows carved on the wall surfaces of the corridors and rooms served as holders for candles and linseed oil lamps, providing both light and heat to the residents.

Because no oil presses have been found inside any underground settlement to date, it is assumed that linseed oil was made outside of the settlements.

The long, low, and narrow corridors restricted enemy mobility. Millstones separating one area of an underground settlement from another provided extra defense. These millstones, which can be opened only from the inside, are 1-1.5 m in height, 30-50 cm in width, and 200-500 kg in weight. Holes bored in the millstones' centers were used to open and close the passageways, visually track enemies, and to allow one to attack with arrows and spears from behind the closed passage. Wooden doors within the settlements, conversely, were used mainly for privacy and were secured by only two or three bolts.

Church/Kaymaklı Underground City

In the Ozkonak Underground Settlement, unlike the others, small vertical holes above the tunnels, next to the millstone, allowed those in the settlement to spear or pour hot oil on their enemies. Narrow tunnels were also set with traps, holes 2-3 m in depth, designed to capture the enemy.

The ground level floors of the underground settlements were usually used as stables. Parts of the stable walls were hollowed out for fodder for the animals. Holes for tying the animals were also carved into the rock.

Warm in both summer and in winter, the kitchens and the wineries are generally found on the upper levels of the underground settlements. The wineries, where wine was made from local grapes, were built on the upper floors so that the grapes could be transported easily. Taking the number of the kitchens into consideration, it is obvious that the kitchens were communal areas. Special ovens called "Tandır" are found in many of these kitchens. This type of oven is still in use in the small towns and villages of Cappadocia. Large earthenware jars used for storing barley, wheat, corn and various vegetables, as well as beer and wine, are also found in the underground kitchens.

Communication holes, no bigger than 10-15 cm in diameter, are found on the floors and the ceilings of the rooms between the various levels.

By using these holes, underground city inhabitants did not have to walk through the long tunnels to communicate with someone on another level. They also alerted underground residents about the presence of danger, so they could take defense precautions easily and quickly.

What they did about the toilet facilities is still unknown. Toilets are found in only two of the underground settlements, Tatlarin and Güzelyurt (Gelveri).

Ventilation and communication shafts generally reach the lowest level of each underground settlement. These shafts were also used as wells. Some of the wells did not have access at the ground level, which prevented the enemy from poisoning the water supply.

Some researchers claim that the underground settlements were connected to each other with tunnels, but no conclusive evidence to support this idea has been found to date.

History

There are prehistoric settlements in the Cappadocia Region, and it is still unknown whether or not these settlements were associated with the underground cities. It is believed that prehistoric man lived in man-made rock shelters consisting of only a couple of rooms. These settlements contain many Middle and Late Bronze Age high reliefs and monuments bearing various inscriptions.

While the Cappadocia region was not one of the main dwelling areas of the Hittites, it is possible to see traces of the Hittite civilization in all of the ancient settlements in the region.

It is believed that the Hittites were responsible for much of the construction and development of the underground settlements.

Underground passages, called "potern," were probably used for military purposes, to defend the Hittite towns. These hidden passages were possibly used for laying in wait to ambush the raiding enemies from behind. Typically, no archaeological artifacts are found in these passages. Some believe that Hittite artefacts were removed by later dwellers.

It is also believed that people of the Roman era played a role in constructing portions of the underground settlements. Roman rock tombs throughout the Nevşehir area are situated near the underground settlements. Everything in these underground settlements dates to the Byzantine Period, from the 5th to the 10thc century A.D. Frequently used for taking refuge for religious reasons, the number of underground settlements increased during this era.

Kaymaklı Underground City

Christian communities took refuge by closing millstone doors when faced with Arab-Sassanid raids, which started in the 7th century. The enemy, being aware of the dangers waiting for them inside, usually tried to force the local people to leave their shelters by poisoning the water supply.

The underground settlements were most widely used during this time period.

It is possible that the Seljuks also used these underground cities as dwellings as well as for military purposes, as the following Seljuk Caravanserais in the Cappadocia Region are only 5-10 km from the corresponding underground settlements: Dolayhan Caravanserai and Til Underground Settlement, Saruhan Caravanserai and Özkonak Underground Settlement, Ağzıkarahan Caravanserai and Pınarbaşı (Geyral) Underground Settlement.

German Martin Urban, who researched the region between 1960- 1970, dates the underground settlements to the 7th-8th centuries B.C., however the earliest source documenting the underground settlements is Xenephon's book, Anabasis.

Xenephon mentioned that the people living in Anatolia and Caucasia hollowed out the ground to form houses, and that these houses were connected to each other with passages. Since Xenephon lived in the 4th century B.C., early dating of the settlements is widely accepted. Despite this research, some people hold that hollowing out the soft tufa by using simple tools would not have been difficult for the people of the Prehistoric Period.

Therefore, there is room to speculate that prehistoric man may have been the first to inhabit the rock dwellings, which were further developed by people of later periods, enlarging the shape, but losing the prehistoric artifacts in the process.

Saratlı Underground City/Aksaray

Used for processing copper/Kaymaklı Underground City

Kaymaklı Underground City

Underground Settlements
Kaymaklı Underground City

Opened to visitors in 1964, Kaymaklı Underground City was built under the Citadel of Kaymaklı, 19 km from Nevşehir, on the Nevşehir-Niğde road. In the village of Kaymaklı, the ancient village of Enegup, houses have been constructed near hundreds of tunnels leading to the underground city. The inhabitants of the region still use the tunnels as cellars, storage areas, and stables, which they access through their courtyards.

The passages are low and narrow, and slope from level to level. Only four floors are open to the public. The first floor is the stable. The small size of this area suggests that there could be other stables in sections that have not yet been excavated. The passage to the left of the stable contains a millstone door, and leads down to the church.

Living areas are located to the right of the corridor. The church on the 2nd floor has a single nave and two apses, a baptism stone, and seating platforms.

The graves on this floor are located next to the church, which supports the idea that these graves belonged to religious people. There are also some living areas on this floor. The 3rd floor contains numerous storage places, wineries, a kitchen, and a block of andesite with various sized carved holes.

Recent research has shown that this stone was used for processing copper. The stone was not brought in from outside, but rather, was part of the andesite layer unearthed while hollowing out the rock. 57 holes were carved into the surface of the stone. Copper ore, about 10 cm in length, would be put into one of those holes and then would be hammered using a hard piece of rock. This technique has been used since the Prehistoric Period.

The copper brought to Kaymaklı Underground City was probably dug from a quarry between Aksaray and Nevşehir. This same quarry was used by the people of Asıklı höyük, which is the oldest known settlement in the Cappadocia region. The 4th floor contains many storage rooms and places to store earthenware jars, presumably used for wine. This indicates that the people living in this underground city were economically stable.

Even though the whole city has not been completely excavated, it is believed that Kaymaklı is one of the largest underground settlements in the region. The number of the storage rooms in such a small area supports the idea that a great number of people resided here.

Derinkuyu Underground City

Derinkuyu is situated 29km from Nevşehir, on the road to Niğde. The city is approximately 85m deep. It contains all of the usual rooms found in an underground city (stables, cellars, storage rooms, refectories, churches, wineries etc.).

Apart from these, a large room with a barrel vaulted ceiling on the second floor served as a missionary school, the rooms to the left used as study rooms. From the 3rd and 4th floors downward, vertical staircases eventually lead to a cruciform church on the lowest floor.

The 55m deep ventilation shaft was also used as a well. Not every floor had access to a well however; some wells were not connected with the surface in order to prevent poisoning during enemy raids. Derinkuyu Underground City was opened to visitors in 1965, but only 10% of the city can be visited.

Kaymaklı Underground City

Derinkuyu Underground City

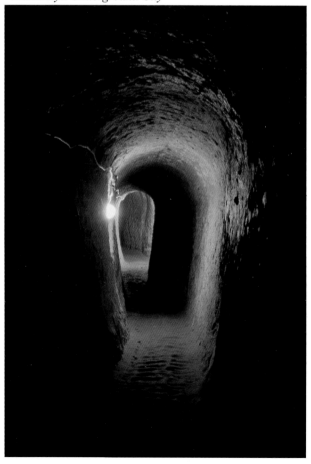

Stable/Derinkuyu Underground City

Church/ Derinkuyu Underground City

Özkonak Underground Settlement

This underground settlement is in the center of the town of Özkonak, 14 km north of Avanos. It was hollowed out of tufa rock, in the western slopes of Idiş Dağı. Although there is only one floor below the ground level, it covers a large area, and tunnels connect the spaces.

Unlike the larger underground cities of Kaymaklı and Derinkuyu, narrow holes (5 cm in diameter) enabled communication between the rooms. When the entrances of neatly hollowed chambers were closed, these holes also served as ventilation.

Unique from other underground settlements, there are small holes in the tunnel ceilings, which were possibly used to pour hot oil on, or to spear, enemy intruders. As in the underground cities of Kaymaklı and Derinkuyu, this underground settlement contains a ventilation shaft, a well, a winery, and millstone doors.

Ozkonak Underground Settlement., visited by thousands of people every year, was discovered by Latif Acer in 1972.

Defence system, Özkonak Underground City

92

Özkonak Underground City

Tatlarin Underground Settlement

The underground settlement of Tatlarin was discovered in 1975. In the province of Nevşehir, 10 km north of Acigöl, it was opened up to visitors in 1991. Although the original entrance to the underground settlement has collapsed, two western entrances remain to provide access to the underground settlement. The underground settlement covers a large area; however, only a small part of it has been excavated. Two floors are open to visitors. In addition to the underground settlement, there are a lot of churches nearby; however, most of them have collapsed with age. The size of the settlement, the number of the storage rooms, and the great number of churches, indicates that this place was a garrison or a monastery complex rather than an underground settlement.

A 15 m curved corridor leads from the entrance to a large rectangular area. A 1.5 m millstone lies at the entrance of the underground settlement. Because three skeletons were found inside the main area, the locals refer to it as a "dungeon". A toilet area and a cellar/kitchen are located nearby. This place may have been used as a graveyard in the Roman Era and as a cellar in the Byzantine Period. The niches in this room match the niches of the Roman tombs found in this area.

Toilet /Tatlarin Underground City

Later, these niches were hollowed out in order to make storage for food. The stable is at the second entrance. This large area, which is supported by columns, was used as a storage room.

There are five storage rooms on the floor of this area. On the ceiling there is a ventilation shaft reaching the other areas in the underground settlement. The first and the second large areas are connected with a narrow passage. In this zigzag-shaped corridor, a millstone door closes both the entrance and a trap door.

Alaaddin Mosque/Niğde

SELJUK REMAINS IN CAPPADOCIA

During the prosperous periods of the Anatolian Seljuks, the Sultans had the settlements connected to one another with a well-planned road network containing bridges, castles, caravansaries, medresses (Islamic religious schools), mosques, and tombs. These foundations were administered by sultans; viziers, and the rich, who had sufficient funds, mainly built these road networks. Although influenced by Arabian and Iranian art and culture, the Seljuks had their own style of art.

CARAVANSERAIS

During the Seljuk Period, the most important three factors in trade were roads, caravans, and inns. The caravans during long journeys, stopped at inns to rest in the evenings. They set off again after having met to their own and their animals' needs.

The first caravansaries, seen in Middle Asia during the time of Karahans, Ghaznavids, and the Great Seljuk State, were buildings called "Ribat." These buildings, first constructed as small buildings for the military, later were developed and changed into larger buildings, used for both religious purposes as well as for inns for travelers.

Especially during the times of Seljuk Sultans, Kılıçarslan II and Alaaddin Keykubat I, the construction of these buildings accelerated and security along the trading roads was provided by the state. Any loss of merchandise was compensated for by the state, a sort of insurance system. During this period, both domestic and foreign trades prospered, and as a result, the Sejuks, already strong economically, became politically strong also.

Traders would be put up for three days in the caravansaries. Their shoes would be repaired, and the poor would be given shoes. The ill would be treated, the animals would be tended, and, if needed, the horses would be shoed. For their religious practices, traders used the "Köşk Mescid," small mosque, in the center of the courtyard.

The "Köşk Mescid," usually located in the center of the courtyard, was the most important part of the caravansaries, typically built on an arched base. The courtyards are normally bordered with a dining room, depots, a bathhouse, and bathrooms. "Mangals" (braziers) or "tandirs" (ovens hollowed in the ground), were used to heat the rooms, and candles and lamps were used for light.

All of these services were provided by the people working in caravansaries, which typically included a doctor, an imam (prayer leader), a depot officer, a veterinarian, a messenger, a blacksmith, and a cook. Stones cut from volcanic rock were used in the construction of the caravansaries in the Region of Cappadocia. For defense purposes, the walls resemble castle walls. Some of the best examples of Seljuk stonemasonry can be seen at the entrance called "Taç Kapı."

Although dragon, lion motifs, and floral designs were frequently used to decorate the caravansary entrances, the examples in the Cappadocia region are generally bare geometrical designs. The doors were made of iron.

Caravansaries were built along roads running from Antalya to Konya to Kayseri to the land of Turkomans, which pass through Erzurum and Tabriz.

They also stretch from the Black Sea region to Iraq, via Amasya, Tokat, Sivas, Malatya, and Diyarbakır, at intervals of 30-40 km, a one-day camel trek. One of the most beautiful examples of a caravansary is in the region of Cappadocia, between Aksaray and Kayseri.

Aksaray Sultanhan

Located 40 km from Aksaray on the Aksaray-Konya road, Sultanhan Caravansary is one of the most magnificent Seljuk Caravansaries, and was built in 1228 by Sultan Aladdin Keykubad. The rectangular courtyard, with a mosque in the center, is entered by way of a splendid portal. Porticos line the right side of the courtyard, while rooms and storage areas are found on the left.

A second portal on the left of the courtyard leads to the stables. Thirty-two piers in groups of eight and four rows in, support the vaults. The only light source inside is a torch-shaped window in the dome.

Karatayhan/Kayseri

Sultan Hanı/Aksaray

Sultan Hanı/Kayseri

The lower floor, access to which is gained by a flight of stairs, forms the base of the turbe. This is the cell-like tomb room where the mummified corpse was either put into a sarcophagus or buried. This room, used for both visiting and worshipping, could have been a mihrap niche, as well as a symbolic sarcophagus. One or two flights of stairs connect to an impressive door.

Besides the polygonal and cylindered turbes, which sometimes have different internal and external plans, there are also examples of square-shaped ones, which emerged after the 13th century.

The ceilings are domed, whereas the exterior has conical or pyramidal shaped roofs. Geometrical and floral decorations adorn the outer surfaces, door, windows, fringes and roof.

The important turbes in the Cappadocia region are the Döner Kumbet, the Hunad Hatun Turbesi, The Çifte Turbe in Kayseri, the Hüdavent Hatun Turbe in Niğde, the Taşkınpaşa Turbe, and the Altı Kapılı Turbe in Ürgüp.

Hüdavent Hatun Turbe/Niğde

Hunat Hatun Turbe/Kayseri

Döner Kümbet/Kayseri

Hüdavent Hatun Turbe

During the Ilkhanid reign in Anatolia, one of the most beautiful examples of Seljuk architecture in Niğde, Hüdavent Hatun Turbe was erected for Hudavent Hatun, the daughter of Seljuk Sultan Rükneddin Kılıçcarslan IV, in 1312 .

The turbe rests on an octagonal base, 80 cm in height. Between the base and the main part is one line of mukarnas. The main part is octagonal, crowned by a sixteen-sided roof. Its wide portal, reachable by two flights of stairs, each with three steps, is on the eastern facade of the turbe.

The door sits between columns and capitals in high relief, decorated with geometrical motifs. Similar columns are found on each corner of the main part. At the upper part, the octagonal main part is divided into two bending outward, turning the octagonal body into a sixteen-sided body.

Döner Kümbet

The Döner Kümbet (conical-shaped roofed tomb) in Kayseri is dated 1276 or later. The marble inscription, consisting of two lines over the entrance, states that it was erected for Şah Cihan Hatun. The turbe, built only with cut stone, has a square-shaped base, an exterior with 12 blank arches, and a cylindered interior. The Döner Kümbet, which resembles a monumental tent, has a conical roof decorated with reliefs.

The facade of the portal bears a relief of a two-headed eagle figure between the figures of two winged leopards with human heads. To the left of the portal, above the date palm, is a two-headed figure with lions on either side. To the right is a date palm in relief.

99

Göreme

CAPPADOCIAN CIVIL ARCHITECTURE

Nineteenth century Cappadocian houses, built on hillsides, were either carved out of the rock or built from large cut stones. Soft volcanic stone, the only architectural material in the region, is easily cut and shaped. It hardens on contact with air to form a very resilient material. The abundance of stone in the area, and the ease of its use, has created a building technique unique to Cappadocia.

Wood is used for courtyard gates and the house doors. Rosette and ivy patterns are used as decorations above the arched doors. The areas between floors are decorated in up to three rows of rosettes, fans, stars, palm leaves, and weather vanes and stylised plant patterns. Windows are grouped in twos and threes and stylized plant patterns are also used as decorative borders. Two types of window are used, either two separately opening panes, or guillotine style.

Both types of houses contain numerous living rooms, a kitchen, cellar, storeroom, an oven (tandır), wine vat, etc. Niches found in the guest rooms are decorated with paintings of vases full of flowers under silken wavy curtains, scenes from nature, or women filling and carrying water vessels. These scenes are painted on plaster.

The most interesting examples of local architecture are from the late 19th and early 20th centuries. Examples can be found all over the region, but particularly in Ürgüp, Ortahisar, Mustafapaşa, Uçhisar, Göreme, Avanos, Güzelöz, nearby Başköy, in the province of Kayseri, and Güzelyurt, near the region of Ihlara.

Mustafapaşa

Ürgüp

Uçhisar

101

CAPPADOCIAN DOVECOTES

Doves symbolize peace and devotion to family in Islam, whereas Christianity regards it as a symbol of the Holy Spirit.

Dovecotes were hollowed out of the upper parts of almost all the valleys and fairy chimneys. The dovecotes generally face east or south. Because doves are in need of water to digest the grains they have already stocked in their craws, they are called "the guarding birds of the fountains." For this reason, dovecotes were hollowed out near the water sources.

Dovecotes were carved, not to catch and eat pigeons, but to use their excrement as fertilizer. The local farmers have used pigeon droppings as fertilizers for generations, which explain the sheer number of dovecotes found in the region. Four or five rows of small niches, or recesses, were carved for pigeons to land on. Wooden perches were also used when needed. Tunnels or ladders were used to reach the dovecotes hollowed into the high cliff.

Some churches and monasteries were turned into dovecotes by closing up the entrances and the windows. Some of the best examples of this type of dovecote are the Çavuşin Church (Nicephorus Phocas) near Çavuşin, the Kılıçlar Kuşluk Church (of Mother Mary) in Göreme, and some churches in the valley of Karşıbucak.

Many of the frescoes in these churches were well preserved because they were not exposed to sunlight. They were also protected from people, as farmers go into the dovecotes only once a year.

Dovecote facades were generally embellished in accordance with the tradition of the time and in harmony with the social life. The dyes were extracted from trees, flowers, wild grass, and soil with ferrous oxide. In addition to this, the red dye, widely used in decorating dovecotes, was extracted from a kind of soil/mud known as "Yoşa" in the region. According to locals, mixing plaster with the white of an egg made a white paint.

Animals, such as martens and foxes, found the painted surfaces difficult to climb, sparing many pigeons and eggs. However, with most of the dovecotes on the western side of Uçhisar castle, a simpler method, tinplate or zinc plates were used. Research indicates that Cappadocian artists who lived in the 18th and 19th centuries preferred motifs that were simple, yet mystical. The wheel of fortune motif adorns both sides of almost all of the dovecotes found in the valleys of Göreme, Çavuşin, and Zelve.

The wheel of fortune is one of the oldest Anatolian motifs. Although in the past it symbolized the four gods of wind, it now symbolizes the world going round, destiny, and the circle of fate and love. The tree of life coupled with a bird and a pomegranate is widely used with the wheel of fortune motif. The tree of life, which stems from Shaman beliefs, symbolizes the way to the other (spiritual) world. The birds guarding the tree symbolize one's company during the journey. The pomegranate, symbolizing heaven, abundance and fertility, has been regarded as a holy fruit through history. It also indicates that the marriage will be blessed, the family will become rich, and the couple will have many children who will have long lives.

In addition to motifs, inscriptions written in old Turkish are also found in dovecotes. Those inscriptions generally bear the date when the dovecote was built. Most common are words such as "Masallah" and "Allah," and occasionally the name and the occupation of the owner.

Although most of the dovecotes in the region of Cappadocia date back to the late 19th and early 20th centuries, there are few examples dating to the 18th century. These small buildings do not attract much attention, but bear Islamic paintings rarely found in the Cappadocia region.

In the region of Cappadocia, the dovecotes are mainly found in the valleys of Göreme near Uçhisar, Kılıçlar and Güllüderesi, the Üzengi valley of Ürgüp, Balkanderesi, the valley of Kızılçukur in Ortahisar, the valley of Çat near Nevşehir, and in the Soğanlı Valley in the province of Kayseri.

SOBESOS ANTIQUE CITY

Sobesos antique city is situated on the Ürgüp-Soğanlı road, 30 kilometers to Ürgüp, in Şahinefendi village. Due to the excavations, the meeting hall and the bath complex have been discovered. The meeting hall is about 400 square meters in size and consist of three rooms. In one of the rooms is a grave and the second one is with mosaics.

The main room is supported by the columns, the floor is covered with mosaics and the walls are plastered. It is estimated that the building was constructed during the middle of the 4th century or in the 5th century A.D. The floor of the mosaic room has been completely cleaned and it is covered with mosaics of numerous colored stones.

The patterns are geometrical with swastika, meander and cross shapes that are made in the forms of hair braid. An open air chapel was constructed on the top of the meeting hall near the east room. It was coarsely built with materials that were supplied from the main hall.

Based on the date of a coin that was found during excavation, the chapel is estimated to be from the middle of the 6th century. 30 meters north of the building, a bath complex of the city with mosaics was completely unearthed.

An apoditorium (dressing room) with mosaics, a caldarium (steam room), and a large section of the cistern that was supported by a semi-circle wall were excavated. It is apparent that the apoditorium had been covered with a 'barrel-vault' roof, but was burned during a fire.

The bath was built with the hypocaust system (hot air heating system). The floor with only the remains of a hexagon marble was discovered with round terracotta 'tondos' supporting it. This building that belonged to the Late Roman Period was renovated for functional reasons during the Early Christian Period.